SCHIRMER PERFORMANCE EDITIONS

SATIE
GYMNOPÉDIES AND GNOSSIENNES

Edited and Recorded by Matthew Edwards

To access companion recorded performances online, visit:
www.halleonard.com/mylibrary

Enter Code
6284-8765-0786-1261

Une baignade à Asnières
(Bathers at Asnières)
(1884, retouched 1887)
by Georges-Pierre Seurat
(1859–1891)

ISBN 978-1-4234-9711-0

G. SCHIRMER, *Inc.*

DISTRIBUTED BY

HAL•LEONARD®
CORPORATION
7777 W. BLUEMOUND RD. P.O. BOX 13819 MILWAUKEE, WI 53213

www.musicsalesclassical.com
www.halleonard.com

CONTENTS

Lent et douloureux *(Slowly and mournfully)*

Lent et triste *(Slowly and sadly)*

Lent et grave *(Slowly and solemnly)*

Lent *(Slowly)*

Avec étonnement *(With astonishment)*

Lent *(Slowly)*

The price of this publication includes access to companion recorded performances online, for download or streaming, using the unique code found on the title page. Visit **www.halleonard.com/mylibrary** and enter the access code.

HISTORICAL NOTES

ERIK SATIE (1866–1925)

"He is the writer of little sets of piano pieces with laboriously absurd titles; wisps of music plastered with facetious directions and descriptive comments." [1]

– Wright W. Roberts, 1923

At 9 AM on the 17th of May, 1866, Eric Alfred Leslie Satie was born on the northern coast of France, in the small town Honfleur. In the following five years, his parents Alfred Satie and Jane Leslie Anton welcomed three other children into the family, and moved from Honfleur to Paris. In 1872, however, tragedy struck the family, and young Eric's life changed dramatically. First, his youngest sister Diana died, only four months old; then without warning, his mother passed in October of that year, at the age of 34. His father, distraught and devastated by these events, felt incapable of raising his three children, and placed them into the care of relatives. Eric and his brother Conrad were sent to live with Alfred's parents. [2] Even this relocation was short-lived, as Eric was quickly sent off to live as a boarding student at the Collège of Honfleur, where he stayed until he was 12 years old.

The return to Honfleur was the beginning of a series of events that would direct Satie toward a life of music. The first of these came in 1874, when he began to study piano. His teacher, a local organist named Vinot, instilled in Satie what would grow to be a deep love of Gregorian chant, and by extension, all things Medieval. [3] Then, in 1878, upon the sudden death of his grandmother, Satie returned to his father in Paris. The move alone might be inconsequential, if it were not that his father had met, and fallen in love with Eugénie Barnetche, a piano teacher and "mediocre salon composer." [4] At her insistence, Eric applied to the Paris Conservatoire.

The Conservatoire was one of the most respected musical institutions in Europe, and gaining entrance was no small task. However, Eric was not happy to be there.

"The Paris Conservatoire offered a music curriculum that differed dramatically from the programme Satie had followed with Vinot, as well as an atmosphere far less inspiring than the eclectic décor at Honfleur. Satie later described it as a 'huge, very uncomfortable, and rather ugly building, a sort of local penitentiary, without exterior charm—or interior, either.' The nation's premier school for the training of musicians had by the late nineteenth century become a stodgy institution known primarily for its rigour and insistence on technical excellence." [5]

Similarly, the faculty had no great love for him, describing him as "worthless" and "the laziest student in the Conservatoire." [6] This conflict between the inspirational and the academic became a critical element of Satie's life. The destructive words of his teachers didn't reduce his confidence, but rather emboldened him to seek out what he believed to be true art. Rather than coerce him to conformity, these years more likely committed him to originality, and ultimately established his independent nature.

Eric's father, Alfred, after having served the government as a translator for several years, rather abruptly decided to change careers. In 1881, at the urging of his wife, he purchased the musical catalogue of a publisher, and began selling the scores. By 1883, he was publishing new works, including pieces by Eugénie, and his son Eric. These early works of Eric's were more traditionally conceived, and may have been guided by the expectations of his parents. His distaste for this kind of conformity led to family difficulties, and by 1887, he moved out of the house.

He moved to Montmartre, an area in the northern part of Paris, and took up residence in an apartment near the famous cabaret, Le Chat Noir. He quickly became part of the cabaret's free-thinking and modern lifestyle, and began to refer to himself as "Erik Satie, gymnopédiste." "Free from his restrictive upbringing, he enthusiastically embraced the reckless bohemian lifestyle and created for himself a new persona as a long-haired man-about-town in frock coat and top hat."[7] In this and other cabarets, he performed on the piano, and composed works for "shadow plays." In addition, he became acquainted with several important artists of the era, most significantly Claude Debussy. They grew to be very close friends, and while Satie may have ultimately had a greater influence on Debussy, the initial beneficiary of the relationship was Satie. Debussy regarded Satie's works very highly, and his orchestration of the first and third of the Gymnopédies provided a strong and early boost to Satie's compositional career.

From this point onward, Satie's career was generally successful, and eventually he was able to write predominantly on commission. He worked with some of the most important artists and creators of the age, among them Diaghilev and Picasso. It is even said that his classical simplicity had an influence on Stravinsky, who particularly enjoyed his work. In 1911, Maurice Ravel, who had once referred to him as a "complete lunatic,"[8] performed some of Satie's early works at a music festival. As a result of this performance, his fame grew, and this period of composition in his career would later be described as the precursor to Impressionism.[9]

His personality was, at best, unusual, and he truly lived the life of the bohemian. In general, he was described as a very witty person, not particularly a "brooding" artist. Likely the first notable aspect of his unique nature was his clothing. Shortly after moving to Montmartre, he was described thus:

One day he took his clothes, rolled them into a ball, sat on them, dragged them across the floor, trod on them and drenched them with all kinds of liquid until he'd turned them into complete rags; he dented his hat, broke up his shoes, tore his tie to ribbons and replaced his fine linens with fearful flannel shirts.[10]

Satie loved writing words nearly as much as writing music. He wrote numerous articles for journals or cabaret leaflets. Often he wrote to attack the conventional artists and critics of his day, and could be quite malicious and vindictive. But his humorous side also came through and displayed a sort of "absurdism" that was popular in the times. The following is an example from a journal article entitled "Memoirs of an Amnesiac," describing his daily routine:

I breathe carefully (a little at a time) and dance very rarely. When walking I hold my ribs and look steadily behind me. I sleep with only one eye closed, very profoundly. My bed is round with a hole in it for my head to go through. Every hour a servant takes my temperature and gives me another.[11]

Satie lived his life inspiring some and infuriating others. The most audacious event in his career would surely have to be the premier of his ballet *Relâche* in 1924. Satie and his collaborators seemed intent on irritating the public in as many ways as possible. The title itself is translated as "no performance," and when the audience showed up for the premiere of the show, the theater was dark. "Outrage" would barely begin to describe the emotion of the patrons. A few days later, the first performance did occur, and was met with general hostility, in part because the production used a backdrop constructed of over 300 mirrors that reflected the light directly into the eyes of the audience.

Despite the many successes he had achieved, the general public seemed to turn their backs on Satie after *Relâche*. In 1925, in declining health, he entered the Hospital St. Joseph with cirrhosis of the liver, where he remained for six months until his death on July 1. Yet even this final illness could not dampen his irrepressible spirit, and it is said that "He died...as he had lived—'without ever quite ceasing to smile.'"[12]

To refer to Erik Satie as merely "eccentric" would be to oversimplify the situation. Defined in the dictionary as "deviating from conventional or accepted usage or conduct especially in odd or whimsical ways,"[13] it does ring true of Satie's life and music. However, a deeper study of his writing would show that much of what is called "odd" or "whimsical" is not necessarily without planning.

Perhaps Satie himself said it best: "Je suis venu au monde tres jeune dans un temps tres vieux." ("I came into the world very young during very old times.")

PERFORMANCE NOTES

Introduction to Satie's Music

Throughout his life, Satie was surrounded with the creative and modern atmosphere that so permeated "La Belle Époque."[14] Dadaism, Impressionism, Symbolism, the Avant-Garde, Picasso, Debussy, Milhaud, the cabarets; all of these played into the life and work of Satie. He was so saturated with the creative spirit of his time, that in some respects, he himself became a symbol of the age.

The pianist Alfred Cortot studied Satie extensively after his death, and came to the conclusion that his compositions fall into three eras:

> From 1886–1895, the period of mysticism and medieval influences; from 1897 to 1915, the years of 'clowning' and eccentricities; from 1916 to his death in 1925, the period of the 'musique d'ameublement' ('furniture music').[15]

Satie fell in love with medieval chant at an early age. He was attracted not only to the melodic contours of the chant, but also to the parallelisms found in Louis Niedermeyer's harmonic settings of numerous chants.[16] The Four Ogives of 1886 and the Three Sarabandes of 1887 most clearly display this focus on melody and parallel chords. Below is an example from the first Sarabande:

The Gymnopédies and Gnossiennes round out the more important works from this "first era."

The "second era" is accurately described by Cortot. The titles alone are enough to make the case, and examples include "The Dreamy Fish," *Three Morceaux in the Form of a Pear*, and "Airs that Frighten You Away." The music, however, is not always as eccentric as the title suggests. Melody is nearly always prominent and carefully

constructed. One of the most beautiful of his works from this era is the vocal song "Je te veux," written in 1900, and arranged for piano in 1901. While not as forward-looking as many works from this era, its melody is quite captivating, and the harmony is rather "traditional." This is surely reminiscent of the kind of salon works that Satie played during his days at the Chat Noir. On the other hand, works like the above-mentioned "Airs" contain carefully crafted melodies, but they exist over a more chromatic and unexpected harmony. Satie's own thoughts on melody seem appropriate:

> Craftsmanship is often superior to subject matter. Do not forget that the melody is the Idea, the outline; as much as it is the form and the subject matter of a work. The harmony is an illumination, an exhibition of the object, its reflection.[17]

Highlights of the third era include *Parade*, *Relâche*, and *Socrate*. The first two of these are orchestral, and the final for voice and orchestra (or piano). While proponents of Satie claimed that this was his finest and most uniquely creative era, others would say that it was the beginning of the end of his success. In this music we find many elements that might be called experimental for the time, including strong hints of minimalism, and neo-classicism. It is, without doubt, a most unusual collection of works, yet it also seems to be a loud declaration by Satie that he will never be contained or stereotyped.

The pace of change in his style left critics and audiences alike rather confused at times, and numerous writings can be found discussing Satie's place in the musical world. As time moves on, he is perhaps seen more as a visionary of things to come, and one who influenced larger figures like Debussy, Milhaud, and Stravinsky. But the sentiment of his own time is reflected best in this comment from an article written in 1923: "Satie, then, seems likely to live as a musical miniaturist. Truly, the man is a problem. Solution will come, but the time is not yet."[18]

Performance Suggestions

There is not necessarily a "definitive" performance practice for the works of Satie; I rather doubt that he would have wanted to be very adamant about how his works are interpreted. As a result, there is a fair degree of freedom allowed to the performer, and each performance can be unique and individualized.

Given the eccentricities of his life and much of his music, one might think it appropriate to allow complete freedom of interpretation, to the point of not even following the composer's instructions. However, such a reaction would be extreme, and logic would suggest that certain stylistic elements must be considered.

Melody

Above all, Satie's music is lyrical, and the melody should always attract our attention first. Good clear voicing and thoughtful shaping of the line is critical at all times. The influence of medieval chant is rather obvious in the works of this book. One of the elements to keep in mind is the non-metric nature of chant, which could be described as a feeling of "floating." This same concept works well with the melodies Satie has written here, even though the Gymnopédies do have a time signature. When playing these works, sing the melody in your mind, and think always of the long phrase.

Feel free to shape the line with a wide dynamic range, and even on occasion to accent an important note or two, lifting it above the line to draw attention.

Harmony

The progressions are not complicated, but can be rather repetitive, either single chords or pairs. It is important then, that the harmony support and generally be subservient to the melody. When the accompaniment is repetitive pairs, give a bit of emphasis to the unstable chord, and a bit of relaxation to the more stable chord. This helps the listener hear that relationship, and clarifies the tonal center as well.

When the chords themselves become slightly more complicated, particularly with an added note beyond the triad or seventh chord, always try to define the purpose of that "extra" note. Is it simply for decoration? Or is it moving to a particular note in the next chord; in a sense, "enhancing" the progression?

Pedal

Think of the pedaling in these works as being more for coloring the sound, rather than simply making the melody legato. The harmony will typically be the focus of the pedaling changes (changing the pedal at each chord change), and for the most part, that will be sufficient. As a result, the melody may sound at first a bit over-legato, or "muddy." Yet this kind of pedaling allows the melody to "swirl around" in the air, possibly reflecting the sound of a chant in a large cathedral. I would be careful not to pedal straight through opposing harmonies, however, as the harmonic progression is still important to the structure of the piece, and the support of the melody.

In places where some change is required in order to clear a certain tone or chord, it would be helpful to use half-pedal, and even quarter-pedal. These kinds of pedaling techniques may be difficult at first, but when mastered, can allow the performer a greater degree of control over the sound.

Fingering and Division of the Hands

Of the small number of fingerings I have added, you may find some that would seem awkward, if the line were to be played legato without any pedal. However, with the type of pedaling described above, fingering choices can be focused more on getting a good sound, rather than physically connecting each line. As for any legato, stay in touch with the keys as much as possible, but don't be completely opposed to moving the hand when the pedal is down.

A predominant element of these works is the left hand accompaniment pattern of a single low note followed by a mid-register chord. Often the chords lie between the staves, and editors must decide whether to put the entire chord in one clef or the other, or to split it between the two. It should be noted, though, that where the chord is placed—and even the direction of the stem—should not necessarily dictate which hand plays the chord. In most cases here, the left hand will play the chords, but there may be a few situations where the performer can choose to play a chord with the right hand. I would recommend that whenever the right hand has the melody, it should *only* have the melody, and not take any of the chords. At cadential moments, when the melody pauses, the right hand could be used to assist the left hand if desired. Any markings in the score as to the division of the hands are suggestions only.

Accidentals

The standard rule for added accidentals in music is that they remain in effect until the measure ends. However, with non-metric works such as the Gnossiennes, there must be some clarification. With more complicated twentieth century works, many editors choose to insert an accidental every time one is required, so as to ensure accuracy. Yet in the Gnossiennes, the melody is in clearly marked phrases, which can be treated as measures themselves. In this publication, therefore, consider that any accidental added to a note will remain in effect until the phrase is complete. Of course, natural signs will be used if the note should return to its original before the phrase ends.

Notes on Performing the Individual Movements

TROIS GYMNOPÉDIES

The three Gymnopédies are likely the most well-known of Satie's works. The slow-moving melody over the repetitive harmony has captivated pianists and musicians since their publication. The name "Gymnopédie" has been researched extensively in an effort to discover exactly how Satie arrived at such a title. Of Greek origin, the etymology of the word references a Spartan festival, part of which included ritual dances, performed by boys or men. There is debate over whether the word implies that the dancers were naked, or simply unarmed.

These works are quite similar in their character, melody, and harmony, but each can stand independently of the others. When played as a group, one gets the impression that they are three slightly different "views" of the same subject, each one giving the listener a slightly different perspective. Thus, an attempt to force them to be significantly different from each other is really not necessary.

With this "Three Perspectives" idea in mind, it seems better to discuss musical issues for the set as a whole, rather than individually. Each work is given the tempo indication of *Lent*—slowly—so the tempos should be more or less the same. Each, however, has a different second indication: the first, *douloureux* (mournfully); the second, *triste* (sadly); the third, *grave* (solemnly). The variation in mood seems minimal, but be imaginative and create a slight difference in the sound of each work.

As stated above, keep the focus on the melody, letting it float lyrically over the chords. Harmonically, I find the second to be the most interesting; as an example, the new harmonic direction that begins at measure 15, and moves to a temporary tonic at measure 17. At interesting and beautiful moments like this, let the harmony be the guide dynamically. That is not to say that it should be more prominent than the melody, but simply that the right hand in this example should follow the direction of the left.

Be careful not to have unintentional accents in the left hand, particularly when leaping quickly from the single notes on beat one, to the chords on beat two. Don't move toward the chord until you are completely finished with the first note; there will be plenty of time to travel to the next beat.

TROIS GNOSSIENNES

The title "Gnossiennes" may also have its roots in Greek, even if it is not literally a Greek word. It may be "some sort of vague allusion to the palace of Knossos in Crete, the scene of the legend of Ariadne and the Minotaur"[19] However, nothing in the music seems to be specifically descriptive of any single event or character. Rather, they may be further extensions of the stylistic ideas presented in the Gymnopédies.

The Gnossiennes are sometimes singled out as the beginning of Satie's move away from traditional composition. This can be seen in the removal of bar lines, lack of key signature, and the inclusion of rather unusual performance indications. Straying from the traditional indications, such as "agitato" or "cantabile," Satie instead uses descriptions that are humorous, odd, and occasionally confusing. Examples include "with great kindness," or "very lost." As much as possible, the performer should try to reproduce on the piano the image that these "word pictures" bring into the mind. Needless to say, those images and their translation to the instrument will be different for every pianist. Such, however, is the beauty of this device! These will be discussed in more detail in the individual works.

Even though these works do not contain time signatures, you will quickly find that there is an underlying pulse, and sense of rhythmic organization. While the removal of the bar lines can definitely help the performer to think of long lines, it should not eliminate all thoughts about the meter. The melody and the accompaniment are still essentially built upon a recurring beat pattern, and the important melodic and cadential points still tend to gravitate toward a strong beat.

Seven Gnossiennes were written by Satie between the years 1889 and 1897. Most of these were published individually, but the first publication of the three works in this book as a set was in 1913. Since then, they have become the most recognizable of the seven.

Like the Gymnopédies, these three also are generally similar to each other in terms of their character, but do contain several small differences that make them slightly more individualized.

Gnossienne No. 1

The grace notes are likely the first musical element that grabs the attention in this work. However, in this mystical, exotic-sounding setting, it is important not to emphasize them too much. Too often, grace notes are played with an accent, or the grace note itself is played slightly longer than necessary. For the recording, I've chosen to play them generally quite close to the main note. In some cases, they are actually played together, but the grace note is released, while the main note is held.

These ornaments contribute additional tonal color to the melody, but do not necessarily always fit into the prevailing harmony. Half-pedal will help clear some of the sounds, while maintaining a beautiful "liquid" sound.

Be sure to think about Satie's comments in the score, and imagine how you can "play" his markings, however odd they may seem. Don't be caught up with the idea that there is one specifically correct way to interpret these phrases; they are ambiguous by their very nature.

Gnossienne No. 2

A clear feeling of 12/8 rises slowly out of this "non-metric" work. The eighths will naturally collect into groups of three, with an expected small emphasis on the first; don't try to eliminate this in an effort to be more chant-like.

Follow the dynamic indications to give the line an appropriate rise and fall. Additionally, many of the phrases are repeated; feel free to use the traditional "echo" on the repeat—or not, as Satie himself would likely be more interested in a performer following his or her own musical intuition, rather than feeling confined to traditional expectations.

Concerning the accidentals, remember to consider each phrase as a "measure," keeping the added flats or sharps until the phrase ends. See the comments above for more details.

Gnossienne No. 3

This should feel like it is in 2/2, with each whole note signifying the beginning of a new "measure."

We also find in this work the most unusual musical indications, even at times rather difficult to translate. One of the most intriguing would have to be "*De manière à obtenir un creux*." The roughly literal translation is "In a way (so as) to obtain a hole." The word "creux" can also be translated "pit" or "hollow," all generally conveying the idea of emptiness. This one phrase alone serves as a testament to Satie's wit, and his unique musical ideas. How does one interpret such an indication? My suggestion for this, and the other indications, is to attempt to reproduce the feeling or initial reaction that you have to the phrase, and not to search for something direct and concrete.

Closing Thoughts

While the works in this book come from the early period of his compositional career, it would still be an excellent exercise to listen to several of Satie's works from all genres of his writing. A very brief list would include the following:

Parade – 1916, for orchestra
"Je te veux" – 1901, Cabaret song
Relâche – 1924, Ballet
3 Sarabandes – 1887, Piano
Trois morceaux en forme de poire (Three Pieces in the Form of a Pear) – 1903 Piano duet

Satie's life and work may not currently hold the degree of attention enjoyed by Debussy, or

Prokofiev or any number of other composers. Indeed much of his music is too rarely played, with the great exception of some of the works in this book. Yet he is remembered for his constant push against tradition, and the expected music of his day. And by so doing, he greatly influenced many who would become the "greats" of the twentieth century. We can only wonder what music might never have been crafted were it not for the "eccentric" ideas of Erik Satie.

Notes:

1   Roberts, Wright W. "The Problem of Satie." *Music & Letters*, Vol. 4, No. 4 (Oct., 1923), pp. 313–320.

2   Davis, Mary. *Erik Satie*. London: Reaktion Books Ltd., 2007.

3   Myers, Rollo H. *Erik Satie* (New York: Dover Publications, 1968), p 16.

4   Orledge, Robert. "Satie, Erik." *Grove Music Online. Oxford Music Online*. (accessed 18 May 2010).

5   Davis, Mary. *Erik Satie*. London: Reaktion Books Ltd., 2007.

6   Orledge, Robert. "Satie, Erik." *Grove Music Online. Oxford Music Online*. (accessed 18 May 2010).

7   Orledge, Robert. "Satie, Erik." *Grove Music Online. Oxford Music Online*. (accessed 18 May 2010).

8   Davis, Mary. "Erik Satie" London: Reaktion Books, ltd., 2007.

9   Orledge, Robert. "Satie, Erik." *Grove Music Online. Oxford Music Online*. (accessed 18 May 2010).

10 Davis, Mary. *Erik Satie*. London: Reaktion Books Ltd., 2007.

11 Myers, Rollo H. *Erik Satie*. New York: Dover Publications, 1968.

12 Myers, Rollo H. *Erik Satie*. New York: Dover Publications, 1968.

13 "eccentric." *Merriam-Webster Online Dictionary*, 2010. (accessed 17 July 2010).

14 The Beautiful Era: a time of peace and prosperity in Europe approximately 1875–1915.

15 Myers, Rollo H. "The Strange Case of Erik Satie," *The Musical Times*, July 1945.

16 Wilheim, Andras. "Erik Satie's Gregorian Paraphrases." *Studia Musicologica Academiae Scientiarum Hungaricae*, 1983.

17 Davis, Mary. *Erik Satie*. London: Reaktion Books Ltd., 2007.

18 Roberts, Wright W. "The Problem of Satie." *Music & Letters*, Vol. 4, No. 4 (Oct., 1923), pp. 313–320.

19 Myers, Rollo H. *Erik Satie*. New York: Dover Publications, 1968.

Trois Gymnopédies
1.

Erik Satie

Lent et douloureux (*Slowly and mournfully*)

à Conrad Satie

2.

Erik Satie

Lent et triste *(Slowly and sadly)*

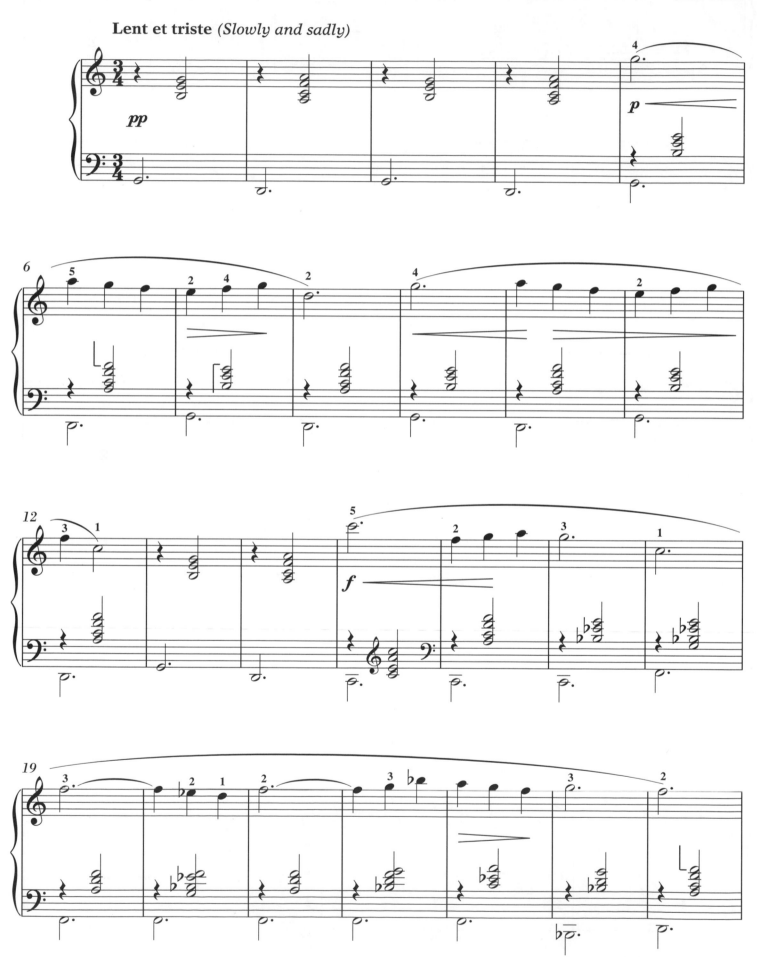

à Charles Levade

3.

Erik Satie

Lent et grave *(Slowly and solemnly)*

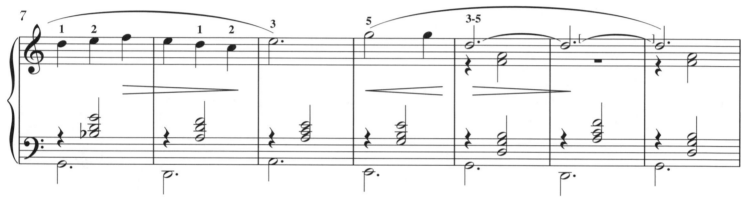

à Roland Manuel

Trois Gnossiennes
1.

Erik Satie

All accidentals carry through an entire phrase (which serves as a "measure"). See page 10 for further discussion.

All comments ("Très luisant," "Questionnez," etc.) are Satie's throughout the *Gnossiennes.*

Du bout de la pensée
(On the tip of the thought)

Postulez en vous-même
(Ask yourself)

Pas à pas
(Step by step)

Sur la langue
(On the tip of the tongue)

2.

Erik Satie

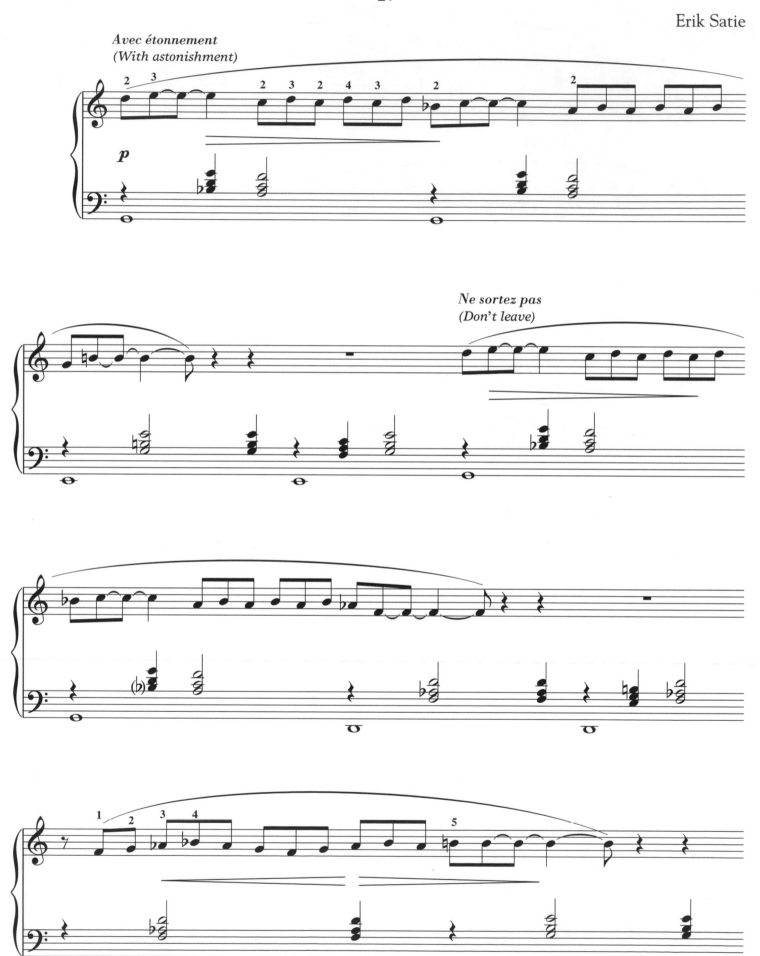

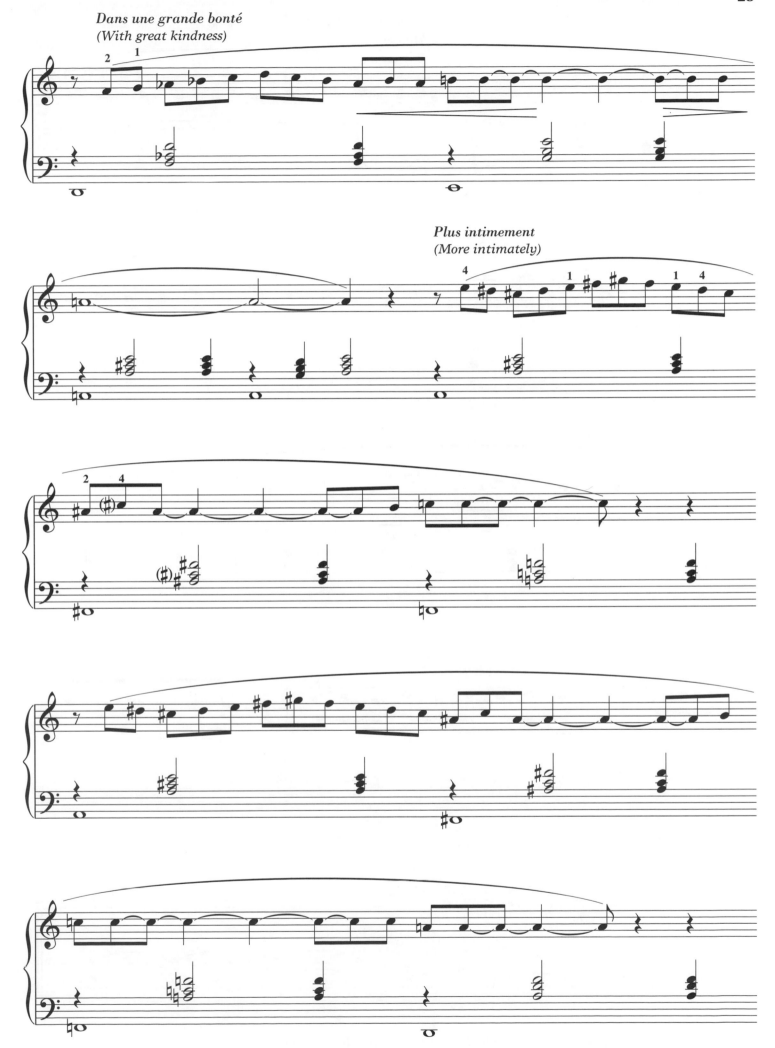

Avec une légère humilité*
(With light humility)

Sans orgueil
(Without pride)

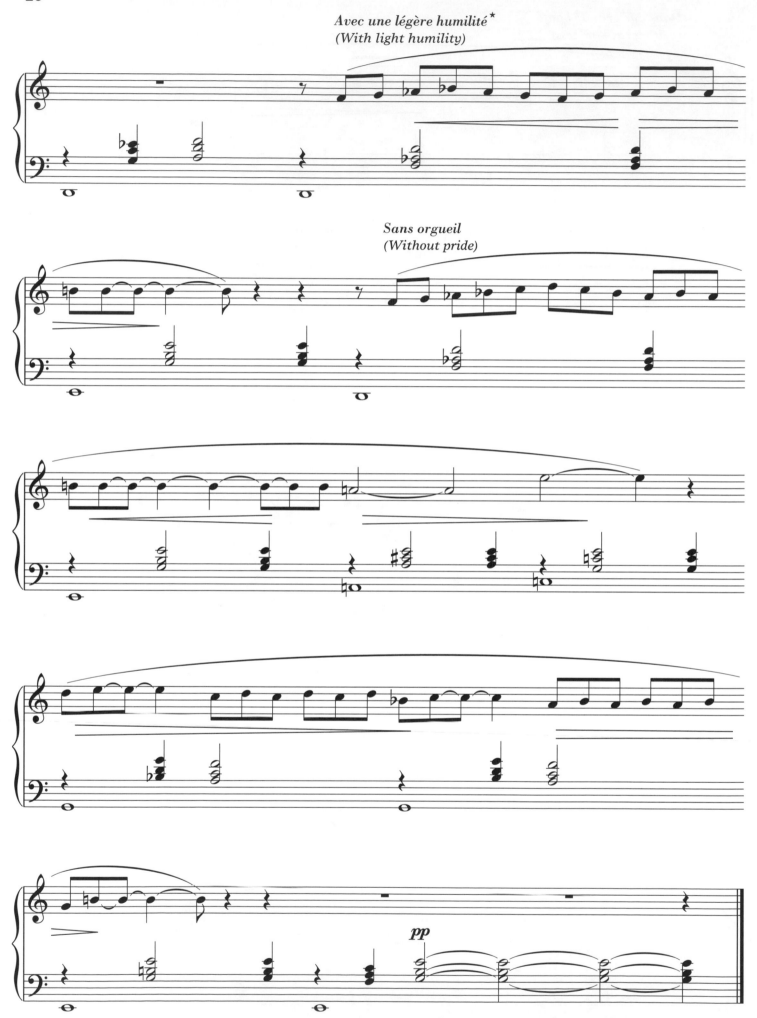

*Several publications indicate "Avec une légère intimité (with slight intimacy)."

3.

Erik Satie

Conseillez-vous soigneusement
(Proceed carefully)

Munissez-vous de clairvoyance
(Arm yourself with clairvoyance)

*This tie is not present in some publications.

Seul, pendant un instant
(Alone, for a moment)

De manière à obtenir un creux
(So as to be a hole)

Très perdu
(Very lost)

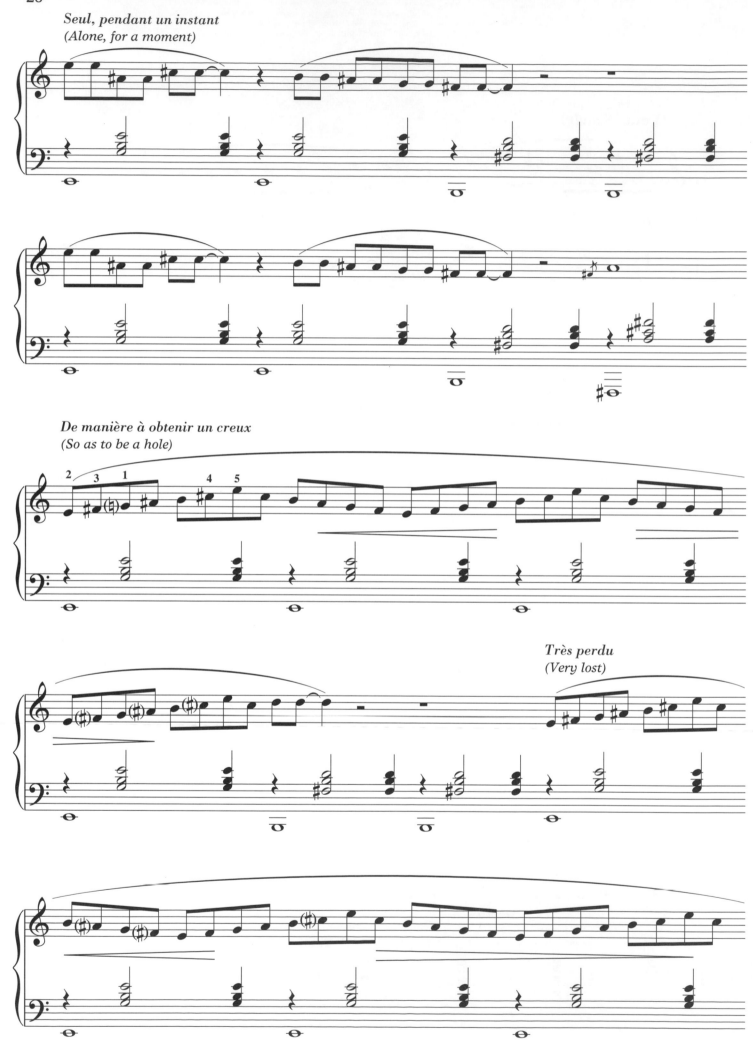

Portez cela plus loin
(Carry this further away)

Ouvrez la tête
(Open the head)

Enfouissez le son
(Muffle the sound)

ABOUT THE EDITOR

MATTHEW EDWARDS

Dr. T. Matthew Edwards is a musician of many facets. As a pianist, he has been hailed by critics for his "...considerable talent...honest musicianship, and a formidable technique." His performances have taken him throughout the United States and to Asia, appearing as recitalist, guest artist, concerto soloist, and collaborative artist. His competition winnings include the Grand Prize in the Stravinsky Awards International Competition, and First Prize in the Music Teachers National Association National Collegiate Finals. He has previously served as part-time faculty at several colleges, including the Peabody Conservatory of Music in Baltimore, and full-time as Assistant Professor of Music at Anne Arundel Community College (AACC) in Maryland. Currently, he is Associate Professor of Music and Director of Keyboard Studies at Missouri Western State University. As a lecturer, he has been featured at the National Conference of the Music Teachers National Association, the World Piano Pedagogy Conference, and at the state conventions of the Maryland, Missouri, and Texas Music Teacher's Association. He also serves on the editorial committee for American Music Teacher magazine. As a composer, he has had major works premiered in Chicago, Salt Lake City, and the Baltimore area, and is a contributing author for the Hal Leonard Student Piano Library. As a conductor and coach, Dr. Edwards has served as the rehearsal pianist/coach for the Annapolis Opera, and musical director for Opera AACC. He lives in Kansas City, Missouri with his wife, Kelly, and their three children, Audrey, Jackson, and Cole.